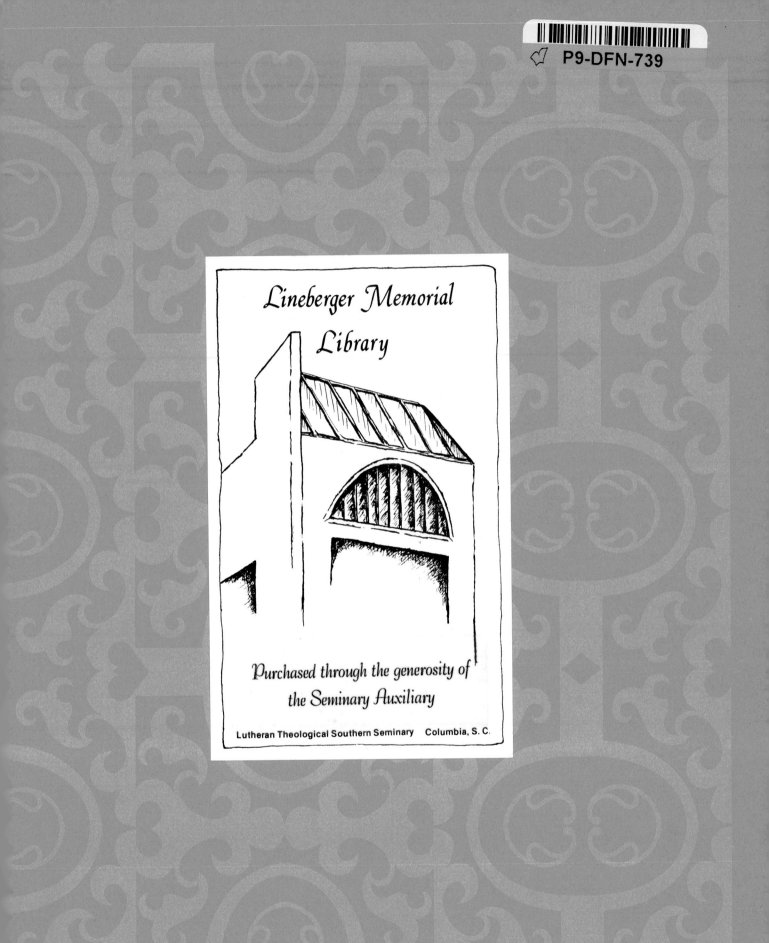

Journeys with Elijah

EIGHT TALES OF THE PROPHET

RETOLD BY

Barbara Diamond Goldin

PAINTINGS BY

Jerry Pinkney

Gulliver Books

Harcourt Brace & Company

San Diego   New York   London

Text Note: C.E. stands for Common Era and is
used to mark the years after the birth of Jesus.
B.C.E. stands for Before the Common Era and
marks the years before the birth of Jesus.

ACKNOWLEDGMENTS

With thanks to Ezra Raanan, who read this collection of stories in manuscript form for accuracy. Like the couple
in the story "A Disorderly Table," Ezra Raanan came to Israel from Yemen via Operation Magic Carpet.   —B. D. G.

Special thanks to Retnata Rutledge for her research,
support, and inspiration for the paintings in this book.   —J. P.

Library of Congress Cataloging-in-Publication Data
Goldin, Barbara Diamond.
Journeys with Elijah: eight tales of the Prophet/retold by
Barbara Diamond Goldin; illustrated by Jerry Pinkney.
p.   cm.
"Gulliver Books."
Summary: Presents eight stories about the
Old Testament prophet Elijah, set in a
variety of time periods and in places
all over the world where Jews have lived.
ISBN 0-15-200445-9
1. Elijah (Biblical prophet)—Legends.
2. Elijah (Biblical prophet)—Juvenile literature.
3. Legends, Jewish.
[1. Elijah (Biblical prophet)—Legends.
2. Jews—Folklore.   3. Folklore.]
I. Pinkney, Jerry, ill.   II. Title.
BS580.E4G65 1999
222'.5092—dc20   96-9278

First edition
A C E F D B

Printed in Singapore

For my editor, Elizabeth Van Doren,

who had a vision beyond mine

——B. D. G.

In memory of Alan E. Cober

——J. P.

Contents

Author's Note

THROUGHOUT THE AGES, Jews all over the world have told stories about the prophet Elijah's reappearance on earth and his working of miracles. These stories abound in the Jewish folklore of Eastern European countries, such as Poland, as well as in Russia and in Asian and African countries, such as Yemen, Morocco, Tunisia, and Egypt.

The prophet Elijah also has a place in the writing and folklore of Christianity and Islam. He is called St. Elias in the Catholic Church and his feast day is July 20. The biblical stories about Elijah are all included in the Catholic Church's scriptures.

In Islam, Elijah's name is Ilyās. He is mentioned in the Islamic holy book, the Koran, as one of the prophets who was sent to tell the people to fear the One God and not to worship other gods. There is a story in the Koran that is very similar to the one in this collection called "A Journey with Elijah."

Elijah is also often identified with the Moslem figure Al Khaḍir, the Green One, who is immortal and can wander through the world unseen. He reveals himself from time to time to rescue someone from grave danger or bring someone a blessing.

The eight tales in this collection come from various time periods in history and a variety of places around the world where Jews have lived. Some of the stories have been set in the times and places of their original sources. Others have been set in times and places different from their origins to give the reader an idea of how and when Jews migrated from one place to another, and of how Jews have lived in places one may never have thought possible, such as China. It is likely that most of the tales set in countries other than their place of origin could have been told in the new setting. The tales surely traveled, just as the people did, from one place to another.

Another reason for setting these stories about Elijah in different times and in different places is to emphasize the age-old idea that Elijah can appear anywhere, anytime, if people will but welcome him and what he stands for—hope and peace.

Part of the appeal of Elijah the Prophet as a figure in religion and folklore is that he is a symbol of hope, a figure who stands for what is just and good in the world. He is a helper and friend to those in need, a teacher of lessons, a master of disguises and surprises. He is immortal, able to appear at any time, in any place, to any person. Because of Elijah's ability to assume any form, the characters in the stories (and we, too) can never be quite sure who he is. He may be that poor beggar on the street or the old man by the side of the road.

About fifteen years ago, when I was deeply immersed in reading and writing about the Jews of eastern Europe, I found myself drawn to the figure of Elijah the Prophet. For a Sunday school event, I even dressed up as Elijah with a beard and old clothes. As Elijah, I greeted each group of children, told them stories, and asked them if they had any money for a poor old man.

Soon after this event, I was home one day when a man came to my door. He was about sixty, simply dressed, and he had parked an old truck outside. He asked if I needed any saws or knives sharpened. I said, "No."

After he left, I was hit with the strong feeling that perhaps I shouldn't have turned him away. Perhaps he wasn't just a poor knife grinder. Whoever heard of a poor knife grinder showing up in this small town anyway? I opened the door to see if I could catch him, but he was gone.

The belief in the possibility of an Elijah encourages us to act as if each person we meet might be Elijah in disguise. It encourages us to be more caring and considerate of others. It teaches us that ordinary people, as well as the prophet Elijah, can help to bring about the days of peace prophesied by the rabbis of old.

The Life of Elijah

IT WAS DURING the ninth century B.C.E., when Ahab, the King of Israel, married a Phoenician named Jezebel, that Elijah the Prophet lived. Queen Jezebel brought the worship of many gods to the royal court and to the people. She was very strong in her beliefs and powerful in her efforts to turn Israel, a nation that worshiped the One God, the invisible God, into a nation that served many gods and cults and that would fill its land with idols and images. She even went so far as to order the prophets of the One God to be put to death.

Elijah, who traveled the land preaching the faith in the One God and denouncing idol worship, angered the royal court. Because of this, he was forced to spend much of his life in hiding—wandering from place to place and living on very little.

One of the greatest of the many confrontations between Elijah and King Ahab occurred on Mount Carmel during a drought that had lasted so long that some people had to sell themselves into slavery to avoid starvation.

On that mountain Elijah issued a challenge. "Summon all Israel to join me," he called to the king, "and all the prophets of your other gods."

When the people of Israel had gathered, Elijah faced them. "How long will you hop from one foot to the other, from this god to that one?" he asked the people. "Today you will witness something that will stop your hopping." Elijah proposed a contest between the God of Israel and Baal, who was the Canaanite-Phoenician weather god and Jezebel's favorite. Elijah continued, "You, who are the prophets of Baal, and I, the prophet of the One God, will each prepare an altar for a sacrifice, but neither one of us will bring our own fire to consume the sacrifice. You will call on Baal for fire and I will call on the One God. We will see which responds."

And so it was done. Before all the people, the prophets of Baal prepared their altar and their sacrifice. They called on Baal for fire. They danced, they shouted, they gashed themselves with knives and spears, but their sacrifice was not consumed, for no fire came.

When they were done, Elijah repaired the altar to the One God, which had been thrown down and broken, and called upon the Holy One. In answer, a great fire descended from the heavens and consumed Elijah's offering, as well as the wood, the stones, and even the earth around it. When the people saw this, they cried out, "The Lord alone is God." Amid the people's shouts came the rumblings of a rainstorm and a heavy downpour. The drought was over.

All his life, Elijah counseled the people of Israel to believe in the One God and to turn away from idol worship. At the end of his life on earth, Elijah passed his mantle of prophecy to his student Elisha. The very last time that Elisha saw his teacher was by the banks of the Jordan River. A fiery horse-drawn chariot suddenly appeared between him and Elijah, separating them. The chariot carried Elijah up to heaven in a great whirlwind.

It is said that Elijah never died. That in Paradise he continues to record the deeds of the righteous and fashions garlands for God from the prayers sung on earth. That he stands at the crossways of Paradise to guide the righteous ones to their appointed places. And that, sometimes, he assumes his physical form to help those in need on earth and to continue to remind us of the presence of the Holy One.

There are certain times that Elijah is especially believed to be present on earth. One is as a guest at the Passover meal, the Seder. On that night the door is opened to welcome him and a full cup of wine placed on the table. A second occasion is at the circumcision of a baby boy, eight days after his birth. There, Elijah is believed to be present as an angel of the covenant, and a chair is often set aside for him. And every Saturday evening, Elijah's blessing is invoked for the work of the new week. It is also said that Elijah will eventually come to help establish peace and harmony in the world.

One

A Journey with Elijah

THIS VERY OLD STORY is set during the third century C.E. in the Jewish communities of North Africa, where Jews worked as farmers, potters, sailors, stonemasons, bronze workers, and traders in grains and oils. Northern Africa, including the countries today called Egypt, Libya, Tunisia, Algeria, and Morocco, as well as the land of Judea to the east, now called Israel, was then under Roman rule. Joshua Ben Levi, the scholar, teacher, and rabbi in this story, lived during the first half of the third century C.E. in the land of Judea. He was among a group of scholars and leaders who were sent on missions to Rome to speak for the rights of his people. In this version of the story, Elijah, who could travel anywhere, takes the rabbi on a journey to the west of Judea, to North Africa.

A Journey with Elijah

RABBI JOSHUA BEN LEVI was a great rabbi, scholar, and teacher, but there were two questions he could not answer: *Why do some people suffer even though they have done good deeds?* and *Why are wicked people sometimes rewarded?*

Each day, the rabbi prayed to God for guidance on these questions. Each day brought no answer. Then one day, when he opened his eyes after praying, Rabbi Joshua saw the figure of a poor old traveler standing before him.

"I think you know who I am," said the old man. "I have come because of your questions."

Rabbi Joshua knew immediately that his visitor was none other than the prophet Elijah. He was overjoyed that his prayers had finally been answered. "I wish to come with you on your journeys through the world so I can understand God's ways," he said.

"It will be hard for you," answered Elijah. "You will see many things that will trouble you."

"But I am already troubled," said Rabbi Joshua. "I will not be a bother to you. Please let me come."

Elijah nodded. "Just one thing. No matter how strange you think my actions are, you are not to question me about them, for if you do, on that day we will part company."

"I will do as you ask," said Rabbi Joshua.

So the two began their journey together, dressed as poor travelers. They walked for days toward the west, through fields and past gardens, orchards, and villages. As they walked they discussed the mysteries of the holy books. Rabbi Joshua was overjoyed to be in the company of the prophet and learned much from him.

Each night, the travelers stopped at synagogues, homes, or inns for lodging and food. Rabbi Joshua saw nothing unusual. Then, one night, as they were nearing the city of Alexandria in Egypt, they stopped at a small dwelling where a cow grazed outside.

A man and a woman came out to welcome them. "We do not have much," said the man, "but we can give you a place to sleep and some food to fill your stomachs."

"I have just made some bread," added the woman. "And our cow provides us with sweet butter, milk, and cheese."

Elijah and Rabbi Joshua gratefully accepted the offer. They ate the good food and slept peacefully through the night. When morning came, they said their prayers before resuming their journey. To Rabbi Joshua's surprise, however, Elijah prayed for the death of the poor couple's only cow! And just as they left the house, they saw the cow collapse in the yard.

"How can this be?" Rabbi Joshua exclaimed. He was overcome with sadness and anger. "These people offer us food and shelter, and you ask for the death of their only animal?"

"Do you wish me to answer you?" asked Elijah. "For if I do, we will part ways."

"No, no," mumbled Rabbi Joshua. "Don't give me an answer."

As he walked next to Elijah, Rabbi Joshua could not help but think about the poor couple. *How can it be that they should help us and be so unfairly rewarded?* he wondered. He felt as confused as he ever had.

Elijah and Rabbi Joshua walked all that day, and at nightfall they stopped at another house. This house was as roomy and richly decorated as the first one had been small and shabby. The owner, however, did not welcome them warmly nor offer them food to eat as the poor man and woman had. Instead, he grudgingly told them that they could sleep outside in the yard.

In the morning, Rabbi Joshua and Elijah awoke and said their prayers. Again, Rabbi Joshua could not believe what he heard. Elijah prayed that one of the wealthy man's walls be rebuilt before it collapsed! As the two left the yard, they saw that the wall had indeed been rebuilt by unseen hands.

Rabbi Joshua walked beside Elijah with questions buzzing in his head. *Why did Elijah pray for a kind deed to be done for the rich man who neither welcomed nor provided for them? Why did he pray for the death of the poor man's cow?*

As confused as he was, Rabbi Joshua stopped himself from asking the questions out loud, for he knew if he did, he would no longer be able to travel with the prophet.

Again the two travelers walked all day, and by nightfall they reached a town with a beautiful synagogue. Benches of gold and silver filled the sanctuary, and the ark contained many Torah scrolls covered with fine fabrics and jewels.

Surely we will be treated well here, thought Rabbi Joshua.

To Rabbi Joshua's dismay, however, the worshipers in the synagogue treated them little better than they had been treated the night before. No one offered to bring the two weary travelers home after the services. Instead, the townspeople spent a few pennies to buy them water and bread. Rabbi Joshua and Elijah had to eat and sleep in the room beside the sanctuary.

The next morning, Elijah and Rabbi Joshua joined the worshipers in their prayers. Afterward, Elijah blessed the congregation. "May it be God's will that you all be leaders."

"How can this be?" muttered Rabbi Joshua, deeply troubled. "Elijah asks for a blessing for such people?" He looked over at Elijah, who was gathering his belongings and making ready to begin the day's journey. The prophet had not heard him, so Rabbi Joshua kept quiet.

The two walked together from morning till night and came to another town with a simple synagogue filled with plain wooden benches and a small but well-cared-for ark. Here the travelers were greeted warmly, invited to a home, fed, and lodged in comfort.

As a parting blessing to these townsfolk the next morning, Elijah said, "May God grant that one of you will be a leader."

On hearing this blessing, Rabbi Joshua could keep quiet no longer.

"You ask for blessings for those who are unkind. Yet the good you do not reward! How can this be?" Even though he was talking to the great prophet Elijah, Rabbi Joshua could not keep the anger out of his voice.

"Do you want me to explain?" asked Elijah.

"Yes," said Rabbi Joshua.

"Then I will. But afterward we must part ways."

Rabbi Joshua nodded.

"First, the poor couple," began Elijah. "I knew that it was ordained for the wife to die that day. Because of their kindness, I prayed to God to take the cow's life instead."

Rabbi Joshua looked thoughtful. "But what about the wealthy man's wall?"

"I knew that the wall was not sturdy and would soon crumble. I also knew that as the man's servants dug a new one, they would discover a treasure buried beneath the house. To prevent this, I prayed that the wall be rebuilt."

"Hmmm," said Rabbi Joshua. "But the synagogue that you blessed with many leaders? Why did you do that?"

"That was not really a blessing, though it seemed so," Elijah answered. "A congregation with many leaders will become divided by quarrels and arguments. But the other congregation, with one good strong leader, will be guided well and will prosper."

Rabbi Joshua was quiet, trying to understand all he had seen and heard.

"God's ways are hidden," Elijah continued gently. "You may see something that you cannot make sense of—a wicked person seems to be rewarded or a righteous person suffers. Know that these things are not always as they seem. Trust God and keep your faith."

With these words the prophet disappeared, leaving Rabbi Joshua with his questions—and some answers.

Two

Seven Good Years

ALTHOUGH JEWS HAVE LIVED in Argentina since before 1754, the majority of Jewish settlers arrived after 1880. Some were from North Africa, the Balkans, and the Ottoman Empire. Most came from central and eastern Europe. They came to escape poverty and persecution, and many lived in agricultural colonies, where they farmed wheat, rye, maize, oats, vegetables, and fruit, and raised cattle as well. Due to invasion by locusts, drought, poor land quality, the isolation of colony life, and the attraction of growing urban areas within Argentina, most Jews eventually left these colonies.

This story is set in Argentina during the late nineteenth century. Since it was a well-known legend among Jews in eastern Europe, it could very well have been brought to Argentina by the new settlers.

Seven Good Years

IT WAS PLANTING TIME, and Julio worked in his cornfield from early in the morning until dark. It was not easy being a farmer in this new land where there wasn't enough water and the locusts came from the north each year to destroy his hard work. But still Julio was grateful for what he did have—his wonderful wife, Mina; five lively children; and his parents, who always told him how much worse it had been in the old country.

Julio bent over the rows with his seeds, as usual. Up and down, up and down the rows he went. But then something unusual happened. There stood before him a stranger where no one had been but a moment before.

Perhaps I have been thinking too much of locusts, and not paying attention to what is in front of me, Julio thought to himself. Aloud, he said, *"Shalom aleichem. Buenos días,"* not sure which greeting to use with this stranger.

"Aleichem shalom. Buenos días," answered the man. "I have come with good news for you and your family. I bring a gift of seven prosperous years. You may choose to have them now or at the end of your days."

"Is it so easy then?" asked Julio. "Poof and there are seven good years. I don't believe it. Please stop your joking and leave me to my planting."

But the next day, the stranger came again. And the next.

This man is not going to give up, thought Julio. So, instead of sending him away on the third day, Julio said, "I will go ask my wife what I should do. Please, wait for me here."

Julio ran home and found Mina feeding the baby with one hand and the chickens with the other.

"Remember that stranger I told you about?" asked Julio, running up to the henhouse. "Well, he's here again. What should I do?"

"This stranger," Mina said thoughtfully, "he could be a joker, a crazy man, even a bandit. But then . . . maybe not. Thank him for his gift, Julio, and take the good years now. We could use them with the children growing up and your parents getting old . . ."

"And the locusts . . . ," interrupted Julio.

"Yes, and the locusts," agreed Mina.

So Julio ran back to the field. The stranger was waiting where he had left him.

"We would like the seven good years now," he said politely to the stranger. "And thank you for your gift."

The stranger smiled for the first time. "If you go home, you will find that they have already begun."

Eager to see if what the stranger promised was true, Julio turned and ran to the house once again. Before he even reached the fruit trees and vegetable garden, he saw his children coming to get him.

"Papa, we have found something in the yard."

"We dug it up."

"A chest."

"Full of coins."

The children and their excitement tumbled around a bewildered and amazed Julio.

When he found Mina, she showed him the golden coins.

"Not a joker or a crazy man or a bandit, your stranger." She winked at Julio. "Something else. A messenger of God, maybe. If we use this gift wisely, Julio, God will continue to look favorably on us. I know."

And though Julio and Mina had always put money into the collection boxes for the needy at the synagogue, they put in more now. Much more. And though Mina had always baked extra Sabbath bread for the elderly in their colony, she baked even more. And she and Julio and the children visited the sick often, though people lived far from one another in the colony and one had to go by horseback from one home to the other. Julio and his family wanted for nothing, even when the locusts came. In this way, the seven years passed.

It was planting time once again and every day when Julio went out to his fields, he wondered if the stranger would appear. He watched for him as he put the seeds in the ground. Up and down, up and down the rows he went. This time Julio was not so surprised to look up from the rows and see the stranger where, but a moment before, there had been no one.

"Your seven good years are over," the stranger said. "I have come to take back your prosperity."

"But . . . but . . . ," sputtered Julio. "Please wait. I must speak to my wife."

The stranger agreed to wait, and Julio ran home.

"He's here, Mina," Julio shouted. "The stranger. He wants everything back."

"Listen to me, Julio," said Mina. "Say this to him, 'We have used your gift well. If you can find anyone who will use it more wisely than we did, we will give it back to you.'"

Julio nodded and took the message to the stranger with a worried look. For seven years he had not had to think about the locusts or the rains or the crops. Would that worry all begin again?

The stranger watched Julio thoughtfully for a moment and then he smiled at him. Julio remembered the smile. "What your wife says is true and wisely spoken," the stranger said. "I know you have used God's gift with care. You may keep your good fortune with my blessing."

With these words, the stranger vanished, leaving Julio as amazed and grateful as he had been on that day seven years before. At once, he ran to the house to tell Mina what the stranger had said.

Mina hugged her husband with joy. "I am thankful," she said, "that the prophet Elijah agreed with me."

Three

A Disorderly Table

THIS STORY IS an old legend that was originally set in Baghdad, the capital of the country now called Iraq. I have chosen to place the story in modern Israel and to set it among Yemenite Jews there. Yemen is located in the southwest corner of the Arabian Peninsula. During the years 1949 to 1950, a large group of Yemenite Jews moved to Israel to escape poverty and discrimination in a country where they were the only non-Muslim religious minority.

Historically the Jews of Yemen communicated with and supported the sages and academies of Baghdad and probably shared their stories as well. It is likely that when the Yemenite Jews came to Israel, they brought those traditional legends with them.

A Disorderly Table

In a village near Jerusalem lived a kindhearted and pious couple who had no children, though they wanted them dearly. Each year when the holiday of Passover came, the couple sat at their table to celebrate. They read and sang and related the story of how the Israelites left slavery in Egypt for the promised land. They couldn't help but remember their own journey from their homeland, Yemen, to their new home in the Holy Land, Israel.

As the years passed, the couple's desire for a child grew, and they prayed for one often. It happened that on one particular Passover, the wife was unable to celebrate the holiday with her usual joy. Once again the couple celebrated alone and the wife despaired that she would never have a child.

The husband tried to soothe his wife's sorrow with words. "Do not worry. We will yet have a child. The Holy One will not forget us."

As the husband was speaking, there was a knock at the door. Surprised, the husband rose and went to see who was there. An old peddler stood in the doorway.

"Come in. Join us," said the husband.

"You must celebrate the Passover with us," said the wife, glad, at least, to be able to fulfill the commandment of welcoming strangers to the holiday meal.

So the old man sat at the table with them. He knew all the words of the songs

and had many stories to tell. The couple enjoyed the peddler's company and were disappointed when he got up to leave.

"Please stay the night," they urged him. "Spend the holiday with us."

"I cannot," the peddler said. "But I want you to know that I will ask the Holy One that I may be worthy of visiting you on Passover eve again next year. I will also ask that when I come again, your table will be disorderly."

The husband and wife were astonished at the peddler's words, and angry. They could not imagine that this man would wish a disorderly table for a couple who had just welcomed him into their house. But they did not say anything; they did not want to spoil their good deed.

During the year that followed the couple forgot the peddler's unkind words, especially since the wife finally became pregnant. Three months before Passover, a son was born.

When Passover eve came again, the couple sat at their table to sing and read and tell stories as they always had. But this time, they held a baby who fussed and cried and had to be rocked and fed and burped and cuddled. Yet the husband and wife smiled at each other. They did not mind. Their table had been quiet for so many years that now they rejoiced in every interruption.

While they were chanting the Four Questions and imagining how their son would chant thus when he was older, they heard a knock on the door

When the husband opened it, he saw an old peddler standing in the doorway. He recognized the peddler immediately as the very same peddler who had visited them the previous Passover eve.

All at once, he and his wife remembered the peddler's words of a year before. What they thought was a curse had really been a blessing. Their table was disorderly, but disorderly with the confusion and joy that a baby brings.

The husband and wife took the man's hands and began to kiss them. They begged his forgiveness for their unkind thoughts. The old man smiled and said, "It is all right. May your son grow strong in the study of the holy books and in doing good deeds like his parents." As soon as the peddler said these words, he disappeared. Only then did the couple realize who this peddler was. He was not just an ordinary peddler, but the prophet Elijah himself.

Four

The Weaver of Yzad

THIS STORY ORIGINATED in Persia, the country now called Iran. Jews came to Persia when their own land was conquered by the Assyrians in 722 B.C.E. and then again by the Babylonians in 586 B.C.E. They fled and settled during these times of dispersion to Egypt in the west, Syria in the north, and Mesopotamia and Persia in the east. Because of heavy land taxes, few Persian Jews were able to engage in agriculture. Instead they worked as artisans, weavers, dyers, goldsmiths and silversmiths, wine manufacturers, merchants, shopkeepers, and sometimes even advisors to the sultan. This story is set in the 1100s, at a time when the Jewish carpet trade was flourishing in Persia.

The Weaver of Yzad

THERE WAS A WEAVER in the city of Yzad in Persia who had a fine business, a family, and a home. He worked hard, loved his wife and children greatly, and always gave to charity.

But one year, the weaver's business dropped off, and he had fewer and fewer orders for blankets, rugs, and fabric. Times became so hard for him that he had no money to pay the people from whom he bought yarn or the people who provided his family with oil, nuts, and flour. His worries grew as his money dwindled.

The weaver became so despairing that he could no longer sit at his loom thinking of his debts and his poor children. He decided to run away from the city.

Before the sun rose the next day, the weaver left his home, his wife, and his children. He walked through the streets of Yzad until he was well past the city. He walked all day, until dark. When he reached some abandoned ruins, he stopped to rest.

The weaver found, however, that thoughts of his wife and children kept him from sleeping. He had not told them where he was going. Nor had he left them any food, or coins to buy food. He could feel his hunger, and it served to remind him of theirs. In running away, he was finding no peace.

Finally, he began to pray.

He had been praying for several hours when he saw a figure pass through the doorway of the ruins. The weaver lay quietly, waiting to see what the stranger would do. Was he a man of peace or one of trouble?

The stranger looked at the weaver and spoke. "I seek shelter, too," he said.

The weaver, relieved, sat up. "These ruins belong to all." He could see now that he had nothing to fear from this stranger, who was old and had a long white beard and a kindly smile.

"And why do you sleep here?" the old man asked, gesturing at the crumbling walls and rock-strewn floor. "You who are still young and strong."

"I am a weaver," the young man replied sadly. "But my business has failed. I could not bear to . . ." His voice faltered and he could not continue.

The old man sat down next to him. "What do you weave?" he asked, his voice low and comforting.

"Rugs. Blankets. Fabric. Mostly fabric," the weaver answered.

"Are there any threads left on your loom?"

"Yes. There are some threads left from my last order."

"This is what you are to do," instructed the old man. "Return tomorrow to your loom. Cover the loom and the threads with a cloth so no one will see them. Then weave. The Holy One will send a blessing through the work of your hands. Sleep now and awake in the morning."

At last the weaver did sleep. The old man's words had brought a lightness to his heart, a lifting of his burdens.

Early in the morning, the weaver awoke. It was still dark. And the old man was gone. He thought of the night, of his hunger and sleeplessness, of the words of the old man. He rubbed his forehead thoughtfully. *It must be that the prophet Elijah came to me in my dreams,* he decided. *I must do all as the prophet has said.*

And so the weaver returned in the way that he had come, in the direction of

Yzad. He was still very hungry, but he was also hopeful. On the road, he met a shepherd with his goats. The shepherd must have seen the hunger in the weaver's eyes. He offered him some goat's milk to drink. After the weaver finished, he continued walking. But the path to Yzad had miraculously shortened in the night, and before the sun was even halfway up in the sky, he could see the city. The weaver sighed deeply and murmured a thanks to the Holy One.

The weaver arrived at his workshop and went to his loom. Quickly, so no one could see, he covered the loom and the threads with a large cloth. He left just enough exposed so he could weave.

The young man threw the shuttle back and forth, back and forth. It was long past the time the threads should have ended. But they did not. The weaver was able to weave and weave and weave, as if the threads had no end, as if he had interwoven the old man's blessing with his work.

He longed to look at this fabric he was weaving and the threads under the cloth. But he did not give in to his curiosity. Instead, he wove all through the night, the blessing making the work light.

Early the next morning, there was a knock on the workshop door. "Where have you been, husband?" scolded his wife. "It's been two days and two nights and not a word from you. Not a slice of bread to quiet the cries of the children. Are you not a husband and a father anymore?"

The weaver hurried to open the door for his wife.

"I am so sorry," he told her. "I felt hopeless. No money to pay my debts. No bread for the children. I was afraid to walk in the streets for fear I would see someone to whom I owed money. I could not come home."

"But I heard you weaving. You must have an order, some money," his wife replied.

"I *was* weaving," he answered. "But I do not have an order or any money."

"I do not believe you," the wife said in anger. She went directly to the loom and pulled off the cover.

The couple stood there amazed. The cloth the weaver had woven through the day and the night was the most beautiful they had ever seen. It sparkled as if jewels were set among the threads, and it felt as soft as baby's hair. Its colors shimmered and reminded them of the beauty of spring wildflowers.

The weaver's wife looked at her husband, a question in her eyes. He smiled. "It's a blessing," he said. And he went on to tell of the ruins and the dream. The husband and wife were both filled with joy and thankfulness.

"Perhaps you can weave some more," she said.

The weaver sat down at the loom, but he saw that the threads had ended and he could weave no more of the special cloth.

"The blessing has passed," he said.

The weaver cut the fabric off his loom and took it to market. As he walked carrying the shimmering cloth, people gathered about him. He had no trouble selling it for a large sum.

With this money, the weaver bought more yarn for his loom and food for his family. He paid all his debts. He worked hard and prospered.

In gratitude for what had happened to him, the weaver decided to rebuild the ruins. He replaced them with a synagogue, a place to pray and to thank the Holy One. Because of this, his story became known for miles around Yzad.

Ever since, the Jews of Yzad have journeyed to this Synagogue of Elijah the Prophet, as it is called. They come in joyous times, during holidays, and in times of sorrow and great need. They come with hopes that their prayers will be answered. The Moslems in the area also honor Elijah's synagogue and bring their prayers to this holy place. And it is said that their hopes are fulfilled, both the Moslems' and the Jews', just as the poor weaver's prayers were once answered.

Five

Elijah and the Three Brothers

THE SETTING FOR THIS STORY is the Caribbean island of Curaçao, which was under Dutch rule from 1634 to 1954. Jews journeyed to Curaçao from Amsterdam as early as 1651. Some of these Jewish settlers were descended from Portuguese Jews who had fled to Amsterdam in order to escape persecution by the Spanish Inquisition, which, under orders from the Spanish monarchy, attempted to force all Jews to convert to Christianity.

The Jews of Curaçao farmed sugarcane, garden vegetables, and fruit trees. They raised livestock, built ships, and engaged in trading. There is also a record of Jews owning a mill to grind corn. These Jewish settlers could have heard this tale in Europe and brought it with them to the New World.

The oldest synagogue in the western hemisphere that still exists is in Curaçao. Called Mikve Israel, or Hope of Israel, it has been in continuous use since 1732.

Elijah and the Three Brothers

A PIOUS OLD MAN who lay dying summoned his three sons to his bedside. "I am leaving you this orchard, my sons," he said. "But you must not quarrel among yourselves, and you must guard it nightly from thieves. If you do these things, all will go well with you."

The three sons agreed. After their father's death, they followed his advice. They were careful to please each other and to take turns watching over the orchard of lemon and orange and coconut trees.

The prophet Elijah saw the good nature of the sons and how they respected their father's last words. One night when the oldest son was guarding the orchard, the prophet appeared before him. Even though Elijah was bent over and his long white beard almost reached his belt, his face had a kindly and youthful look.

"I have come to reward you for the respect you have shown your father," the prophet said in a voice so powerful and deep that it surprised the oldest son. "Do you choose knowledge of the Torah, great wealth, or a good wife?"

The oldest son looked about him. *What I could do with a fortune!* he thought. *I could build each of us a fine house, enlarge the orchard, and . . .* He looked at the prophet. "I choose great wealth," he said.

Elijah handed him what seemed an ordinary coin. But, in the years to come, this coin brought the oldest son good fortune in all his business matters and he became wealthy.

On the next night, Elijah appeared before the second son and offered the same three choices. The second son thought of the joy he felt when he studied his books and wished for knowledge of the Torah.

So Elijah gave him a book that looked like any other. But, when the second son studied the book in the years to come, he became wiser and wiser in the ways of the Torah.

On the third night, Elijah appeared before the youngest son. "To reward you for the way in which you have followed your father's advice, I offer you one of these—knowledge of the Torah, great wealth, or a good wife."

"I choose a good wife," said the third son, who longed for a companion to share his life.

"To fulfill your wish," said Elijah, "we must go on a journey."

The youngest son took leave of his brothers and followed the prophet Elijah that day through fields and over hills and through a village, until they came to a large farmhouse.

When they knocked on the farmhouse door and stepped inside, they saw that the farmer had a daughter of marriageable age.

"May we sleep outside for the night?" Elijah asked the farmer. "We could make our beds in the barnyard."

The farmer agreed and the two travelers bedded down on the straw.

But the youngest son could not sleep. "Is the farmer's daughter to be my wife?" he asked the prophet. He thought her pretty and young and bright looking.

"I will know in the morning," answered Elijah. "Now go to sleep."

As soon as the third son fell asleep, Elijah sat up and began to listen to the cackles of the chickens and the squawks of the geese. To Elijah these were more

than just cackles and squawks, for he could make sense of the speech of animals. And he knew just how much chickens and geese love to gossip and to complain.

He heard one chicken cackle, "Can you imagine! She kicked me out of her way when she brought in the food today."

"At least she fed you," squawked the goose. "What a bad temper that one has. And so forgetful."

The animals were talking about none other than the farmer's daughter. So when the third son awoke the next morning, Elijah told him they must continue their search. "This one is not the companion for you," he said.

Elijah and the third son traveled all that day until they came to a mill for grinding corn. When they knocked on the door and stepped inside, they saw that the miller had a young daughter. The youngest son thought her as pretty and lively as the farmer's daughter.

Once again, Elijah asked permission for the two travelers to sleep near the henhouse. The miller agreed.

After the youngest son fell asleep, Elijah listened to the chickens and the geese cackling and squawking.

"Cackle, cackle." A chicken pecked its way over to a goose. "What a lazy daughter! Don't you think? Doesn't even do her chores until late afternoon."

"Nasty and wasteful, too," the goose squawked. "Breaking my eggs for no good reason but the sport of it."

Elijah learned much more about the running of the mill from the cackles and squawks. And when the youngest son awoke, he told him, "This miller's daughter is not the one for you. We must travel still."

And so that day they walked and walked until they reached a small village and stopped at the shop of a blacksmith. He too had a young and pretty daughter.

"May we stay in your barn for the night?" Elijah asked.

"Surely," the blacksmith agreed.

As they bedded down with the animals, Elijah listened to the chickens and the geese. Peck, peck. Cackle, cackle. The sounds were happy sounds.

"What a lucky man he will be who marries our fine mistress, squawk, squawk, squawk," said the goose.

"A kinder lady no one will find, cackle, cackle," replied the chicken.

Our journey is over, thought Elijah.

The next morning when the youngest son awoke and looked up at Elijah, the prophet smiled. "We have found you a companion to share your life," he said.

"How is it?" said the third son. "She seems no different than the farmer's daughter or the miller's daughter."

But she was. And the youngest son wed the blacksmith's daughter. As each year passed they grew to love each other more and more. Their lives were filled with companionship and joy.

And all three brothers lived near one another by the orchard of lemon and orange and coconut trees, being careful to follow their father's advice. If the three brothers had owned chickens and geese, and if Elijah the Prophet had slept in the barnyard, he would probably have heard, "Cackle, cackle. Their father would be proud of them."

"Squawk, squawk. They are justly rewarded."

And for chickens and geese, who are used to complaining and gossiping, these would be fine words of praise, indeed.

Six

The Fragrance of Paradise

WHEN THE BABYLONIANS conquered Judea, the land now called Israel, in 586 B.C.E., many Jews were transported to Babylon and others fled to Egypt. They continued to live in these places for many centuries. What was once Babylonia is now part of the country called Iraq.

Rabbah ben Avuha was a scholar who lived in Babylonia in the second half of the third century C.E. This story, which is set during the time that he lived, is recorded in the Babylonian Talmud, a body of teachings compiled by rabbis from 200 B.C.E. to 500 C.E. The Talmud is the second most sacred Jewish text after the Bible.

The Fragrance of Paradise

The prophet Elijah often appeared to visit with people of wisdom in order to teach and study with them. On one such visit to Rabbah ben Avuha, while discussing specific points of Jewish law, Elijah was surprised to discover that the Rabbi was not familiar with some very important books.

Rabbah was embarrassed by this, but he defended himself, saying, "I am so poor, I cannot afford to buy books. And I barely have time to study; I must work very hard every day."

Elijah was thoughtful for a moment. Then he said, "Close your eyes, Rabbah. I am going to take you on a journey. You must not open your eyes until I tell you."

As Rabbah closed his eyes, he sensed the light touch of Elijah's hand on his shoulder. Although he stood still, he felt as if the earth moved below him. A wind blew around his face and body, and he felt as light as a goose feather. Dancing colors and flashes of white light filled his head.

When the movement around him stopped, Rabbah noticed a new sensation, a smell. It was a beautiful, clear, strong smell such as he had never experienced before. It was the sweet smell of flowers, of exotic perfumes, of spices simmering in a stew in the oven. Rabbah inhaled the smell until it filled every bit of him with a feeling of pure joy. He felt like singing and dancing and running and shouting.

It was then that Elijah said, "You may open your eyes, Rabbah." Rabbah looked about him. He was in a lush garden. Tall, full spice trees—cinnamon, nutmeg, and clove—abounded. Myrtle and rosebushes added their beauty, too. Streams of wine and honey gurgled past, while golden vines studded with pearls as shiny as the stars surrounded him.

The smell was even stronger now, stronger than he had ever known a smell to be. It was heady and fragrant, as if thousands of roses had been crushed and mixed with sweet spices, with honey, and with wines. The air about him resonated with pure, melodious sounds, as of dozens of angels singing, first loudly, then softly, then loudly again. *I must be in Paradise,* Rabbah thought.

"You are," Elijah answered aloud. "Now, take off your robe, and fill it with leaves from the myrtle bushes. You may bring them back with you. You will be able to sell them at the marketplace for a high fee. Then you will have the money to support yourself and your family while you study all the important books."

Rabbah began to gather the wondrous-smelling leaves into the folds of his robe. But suddenly a deep, resonating voice filled the garden. The rabbi paused. The voice was not Elijah's.

"You can gather these leaves if you desire, Rabbah ben Avuha," the voice said. "But a person cannot take away part of Paradise without losing something later. Do you wish to sell your share of Paradise now?"

Rabbah dropped all the leaves and looked at Elijah. "I cannot bring these leaves back with me, Elijah. I do not wish to use my portion of Paradise in this world," he said.

Elijah nodded. "I understand," he replied.

After checking to see that his robe was empty, Rabbah took a last look at the garden. Then he closed his eyes again, preparing for his return journey. Once more Elijah touched his shoulder, and Rabbah felt as if he were floating.

When Rabbah opened his eyes again, he was in the house of study. Elijah was gone, but the sweet smell of Paradise still lingered in the air. The smell was so strong that soon everyone in the house of study was gathered about Rabbah.

"Where have you been?"

"What do you have that smells so sweet?"

There were questions and comments and feelings of lightness and joy.

"The smell. It is on you, Rabbah."

"It is your robe!"

Rabbah sniffed his robe. The smell of the heavenly myrtle leaves had permeated the fabric of his robe. He had brought the fragrance of Paradise with him, though not his share in the world to come. *Had the prophet Elijah known this would be so?* Rabbah wondered.

The others offered Rabbah large sums of money for his robe, which he sold. No longer was he too poor to study. Now Rabbah could devote himself to learning from the holy books. He did not miss his robe, for the scents of the spice trees and myrtle bushes, the rivers of wine, and the golden vines remained with him always.

Seven

The Blessing

I HAVE ADAPTED this very popular story told by Jews and non-Jews alike in Europe to a setting in seventeenth-century Kaifeng, China, where about 750 Jews lived. The names in this story are authentic Chinese Jewish names. Jews had settled in China by the eighth century C.E. Some came via caravans from Persia across central Asia. Others traveled by sea along the trade routes. They came to escape persecution in Persia or because they were involved in the silk trade.

The Jews in China worked as farmers, shopkeepers, and artisans. They served in the army and the civil service. In general, the Chinese were tolerant of other religions in their midst. Gradually, over a period of seven hundred years, the Jews intermarried and stopped practicing their religion. But there are still people who know they are of Jewish descent living in China today.

The Blessing

IN THE CITY OF KAIFENG, there were once two brothers. The older one, Li Chên, was rich and miserly; the younger, Li Sheng, was poor and kind.

Late one morning, Elijah came to the rich brother's house dressed as an old beggar. He knocked and when the door was opened, he asked for some coins. The servant closed the door quickly, saying as he did so, "My master does not give away his money to every beggar coming up this walk."

That same day, Elijah knocked on the door of the second brother's house. Li Sheng opened the door and smiled when the beggar asked him for some coins. "Of course, of course," he said. "But first, you must come in and share my rice and soup."

Elijah agreed and after eating the simple meal with Li Sheng, he told him, "You will be rewarded for being so generous and kind. The first thing you do shall be blessed and will not end until you call out 'Enough!'" Then he left.

The poor brother did not give much thought to the beggar's blessing. After all, Elijah had looked like no more than an ordinary beggar. Since Li Sheng and the beggar had finished every morsel of food left in the house, Li Sheng needed to go to the market to buy more rice. He began to count the few coins he had left. As soon as he counted a coin, however, another appeared instantly from out of the air. And another. And another.

First Li Sheng stared. Then he smiled, remembering the beggar's words. Then he laughed and danced and counted coins the whole day through and all of the night, too, until he was exhausted.

As the sun rose, Li Sheng cried out, "Enough!" And it was enough, for the pile on the table had spread to the floor and all through the little house. Li Sheng was now wealthy.

Later that day, the two brothers met at the marketplace.

Li Chên watched as his brother went from stall to stall purchasing first some chickens, then some feed for the chickens, and even a pair of golden candlesticks.

"Has your luck changed, Younger Brother?" Li Chên asked, for how else could Li Sheng afford more chickens for his coop and expensive candlesticks for his table, candlesticks that were even more beautiful than Li Chên's own?

Li Sheng turned to his brother, his arms filled with his purchases. "Yes. An amazing thing has happened, Older Brother." And he told Li Chên the whole story of the beggar and the blessing.

That's easy enough, thought Li Chên. *I will do the same and grow even wealthier than I already am.* He left the marketplace in a hurry, determined to watch for the old beggar. He, too, would answer the door and offer him rice and soup and coins. He, too, would receive the beggar's blessing.

Li Chên did not have to wait long. The very next day, he saw the old beggar pass by his house.

Li Chên ran outside. "Wait. I am so sorry my servant did not let you in the other day. Please come with me. I have some rice and soup to feed you. And some coins to give you."

The beggar joined Li Chên and walked into his house.

"What a fine home you have," said the beggar.

Li Chên nodded, enjoying the compliment. "Here, at the table is the rice and soup," he said.

"Will you not join me?" asked the beggar.

"Oh"—Li Chên waved his hand—"go ahead. I've already eaten."

So the beggar ate. When he was finished, Li Chên gave him a few coins. "Many thanks," said the beggar. "May the first thing you do have no end, until it is enough." And the beggar left.

Li Chên was so happy. *Now I will count my coins too, just as Younger Brother did, and they will fill my house,* he thought.

Li Chên pulled a chair over to the table so he could count in comfort for as long as possible. But sit in it he could not. The chair seemed glued to his hand.

Li Chên pushed on the chair.

He pulled on it.

He knocked it.

He banged it.

Still the chair remained attached to his hand. Li Chên was forced to pull and push, push and pull on the chair over and over again. Finally, he cried, "Enough!"

And this is how the rich and miserly brother, Li Chên, wasted the prophet's blessing in his greediness for even more gold.

Eight

Meeting Elijah

THIS STORY ORIGINATED in the nineteenth or early twentieth century in eastern Europe, where it is set. Jews fleeing persecution in Germany fled eastward to Poland, Lithuania, and Russia as early as 1069 C.E. From the thirteenth century on, more and more Jews arrived, as a result of protective charters granted by various rulers, such as Casimir the Great and the Grand Duke Witold. This golden age of Polish Jewry ended in 1648 with the Cossack revolt and its aftermath.

The German language that the original immigrants spoke became transformed over the centuries of living in eastern Europe into a language called Yiddish, which is written with Hebrew letters and contains words from German as well as Hebrew and several other languages.

Meeting Elijah

O<small>N A SATURDAY AFTERNOON</small> in the study hall in Trusk, Rabbi Meir sat with his students. It was getting close to the holiday of Passover, a time when people's thoughts turned to the prophet Elijah. For it is on this holiday that they hope Elijah will come, and with his visit, bring peace.

It was rumored in Trusk that Rabbi Meir had actually seen Elijah, even talked to him. And now the rabbi's students begged him to tell them about it.

"Did you really see Elijah?" asked one.

"What did he look like?" inquired another.

"What did he say?" questioned a third.

"Ssh," said Rabbi Meir. "And I will tell you how it was."

The hall quieted and the rabbi began. "Many times, when I was a boy, I would see my father struggling with a difficult question concerning the holy books. Day after day he would struggle. Then one day, he would come with shining eyes and explain the answer in a clear and extraordinary manner.

"At those moments, I gazed at my father in awe. And my father would say, 'It was Elijah the Prophet who instructed me.'

"This happened again and again, until finally I begged him, 'Please, Father. Could I also see Elijah the Prophet?'

"My father would not agree. I begged over and over.

"At last my father said, 'You must fast for forty days. You may eat and drink only at night. During the forty days, you must study the holy books to prepare yourself. Your eyes must not stray from the books. Then, on the fortieth night, you will see Elijah.'

"I was overjoyed at the news. But it took me years before I was able to do as my father instructed. All that time, I did not forget his words, nor did my desire to see the prophet diminish. Only a few years ago, with great effort and suffering, did I manage to fast and study for forty days.

"On the fortieth night, I went to my father.

"'I have done as you've said. I have fasted and studied.' I told him.

"'Then go to the study house,' my father instructed. 'Light all the lamps and study all night. Try to study there alone and Elijah the Prophet will appear to you.'

"Eagerly I walked from my father's house to the house of study. My anticipation warmed me, though it was bitter cold outside. When I opened the study door, however, I stopped abruptly. The room was full of people poring over the holy books, studying alone and in small groups.

"I did not say a word and by ten o'clock, as I had hoped, most of my companions had left. I persuaded one, then another of the ones who remained to leave.

"'Yonkel,' I said, 'I think your wife is waiting up to see you. Leyzer, shouldn't you go to bed already? You have to get up early to milk your cows.'

"Finally, I was alone. I breathed deeply, relieved for the first time that evening. At any moment Elijah would surely come.

"I sat down at one of the long tables laden with books and chose to study an old tattered one that was a favorite of my father's. I could not relax, but sat straight in my chair, waiting. I could hear the ticking of the big old clock and the pounding of the wind against the walls of the building.

"Suddenly I heard a knock. I was surprised, as I did not expect Elijah to come in by the door, just as any ordinary person would.

"I opened the door and was dismayed to see Izzy the glass cutter standing there. He walked past me, over to the stove to warm himself.

"'Well, it is not that late,' I said to myself, and went back to my studying. Every once in a while, I would glance over at Izzy, who still sat by the stove, his head heavy and nodding with sleep. I was worried. I knew that Izzy often stayed all night by the stove because his cottage was so small and cold.

"I woke him and said, 'Izzy, you must go home. The study house is closed for the night.'

"'Closed! The study house has never been closed before!' Izzy protested. He did not budge.

"'Tonight it is closed,' I said. 'I am sorry, but I must study here all alone.'

"'I never heard of such a thing! I will tell your father of this tomorrow!' Izzy shouted at me as he left for his cottage.

"I locked the door. Surely Elijah could enter even if the door was locked, I thought.

"I felt tired and weak from the fasting, but I was still eager to see the prophet. I sat down, and there was another knock on the door. I groaned. Who was it this time? I had no more patience.

"I opened the door. It was not Izzy the glass cutter again, as I had expected. No, this time it was a peddler, a stranger. His clothes were patched and he carried many packages on his back. He began to put the packages down inside the door.

"'This is not an inn for wandering peddlers,' I said, stopping him. 'You cannot stay here tonight.'

"The peddler sighed. 'If you send me back out into the cold, it will surely mean my end,' he said.

"'You will have to find other lodgings,' I insisted, and closed the door. I returned to my study of the holy books.

"The winter winds continued to blow outside. I could hear them knocking against the window. But I did not think of the glass cutter or the peddler. All that was on my mind was Elijah.

"The clock sounded. It was twelve o'clock. Surely Elijah would come now. The winds quieted. The clock struck one o'clock. Then two. I still awaited the great prophet, certain he would come. Hadn't I fasted and studied and done all my father had instructed?

"Three. Four. I began to doze, my head falling toward the holy book before me. I got up and walked over to the window. It was still black outside. I put my forehead against the frosted windowpane, feeling its coldness to keep awake.

"Five. Six. Suddenly there was a knock on the door. I flew to open it, wide awake and eager once again. But it was only members of the study house come early to say the morning prayers before going to work. I prayed with them and then went to see my father.

"'Did you see Elijah?' my father asked as soon as I walked into his study.

"'No,' I answered, very disappointed. 'He did not come. I stayed awake studying alone the whole night, as you told me.'

"'Didn't a peddler burdened with packages come to the door?' asked my father.

"'Well, yes,' I said. 'I sent him away so I could be alone.'

"'You sent away Elijah the Prophet,' my father said, shaking his head. 'That was the way he first appeared to me. As a poor peddler in need of a warm place to spend the night.'

"'But, Father, I made everyone leave because of you. You said for me to study alone.'

"'How could you think I would order you to drive a poor peddler out into the cold? Do you think by doing so, you would be worthy to see the great prophet?' he replied. His face looked old and tired."

"And so, you see," Rabbi Meir said to his students, "I did see Elijah. But I did not recognize him, nor was I worthy of sitting and studying with him as my father does.

"I have not seen the prophet since that time," the rabbi continued. "But now I greet each person I meet with a full heart no matter how he or she looks or who he or she is. In this way, I hope to be worthy of meeting the great prophet once again, and this time of not turning him away."

For Further Reading

ABOUT THE LIFE OF ELIJAH:

Augustinović, A. *"El-Khadr" and the Prophet Elijah*. English translation by Eugene Hoade. Jerusalem: Franciscan Print. Press, 1972.

"Elia (Elijah)." *New Catholic Encyclopedia*. Vol. V. New York: McGraw-Hill Book Co., 1967.

"Elijah." *Encyclopedia Judaica*. Vol. 6. Jerusalem: The Macmillan Co., 1971.

"Elijah." *The Jewish Encyclopedia*. Vol. V. New York: KTAV Publishing House, Inc., 1964.

"Ilyas." *The Encyclopedia of Islam*. Vol. II. Leiden: Late E. J. Brill Ltd. Publishers and Printers, 1927.

Tanakh: A New Translation of the Holy Scriptures According to the Traditional Hebrew Text. Philadelphia: The Jewish Publication Society, 1985.

ABOUT THE STORIES:

Ausubel, Nathan, editor. *A Treasury of Jewish Folklore: Stories, Traditions, Legends, Humor, Wisdom and Folk Songs of the Jewish People*. New York: Crown Publishers, 1948.

Bin Gorion, Micha Joseph. *Mimekor Yisrael: Classical Jewish Folktales*. 3 vols. Collected by bin Gorion, Emanuel, editor. English translation by I. M. Lask. Bloomington: Indiana University Press, 1976.

Epstein, Rabbi I., editor. *The Babylonian Talmud*. London: Soncino Press, 1935–48.

Frankel, Ellen. *The Classic Tales: 4,000 Years of Jewish Lore*. Northvale, N.J.: Jason Aronson, Inc., 1989.

Gaster, Moses. *The Exempla of the Rabbis: Being a Collection of Exempla, Apologues and Tales Culled from Hebrew Manuscripts and Rare Hebrew Books.* New York: KTAV Publishing House, Inc., 1924, 1968.

Ginzberg, Louis. *The Legends of the Jews.* Vol. I. Philadelphia: The Jewish Publication Society of America, 1909, 1937.

Hechal, Edna, IFA Coordinator. Israel Folktale Archives (IFA). Haifa, Israel: University of Haifa (story "The Weaver of Yzad," translated from the Hebrew for me by Alisa Klein).

Klapholtz, Yisroel Yaakov. *Stories of Elijah the Prophet.* Part I. English translation by Abigail Nadav. Jerusalem: Feldheim Publishers, 1970.

————. *Stories of Elijah the Prophet.* Parts II and IV. English translation by Abigail Nadav. Bnei Brak: Pe'er Hasefer Publishers, 1971.

Sadeh, Pinhas. *Jewish Folktales.* English translation by Hillel Halkin. New York: Doubleday, 1989.

Schram, Peninnah. *Tales of Elijah the Prophet.* Northvale, N.J.: Jason Aronson, Inc., 1991.

Schwartz, Howard. *Miriam's Tambourine: Jewish Folktales from Around the World.* New York: Seth Press, 1986.

ABOUT THE LOCATIONS OF THE STORIES:

de Lange, N. R. M. *Atlas of the Jewish World.* New York: Facts on File, Inc., 1992.

Emmanuel, Isaac Samuel, and Suzanne A. Emmanuel. *History of the Jews of the Netherlands Antilles.* Cincinnati: American Jewish Archives, 1970.

Gilbert, Martin. *The Atlas of Jewish History.* New York: William Morrow & Company, Inc. 1969.

Leslie, Donald. *The Survival of the Chinese Jews: The Jewish Community of Kaifeng.* Leiden: E. J. Brill, 1972.

Matchan, Linda. *The Ancient Jews: How They Lived in Canaan.* Vancouver, Canada: Douglas & McIntyre Ltd., 1980.

Pollak, Michael. *Mandarins, Jews, and Missionaries: The Jewish Experience in the Chinese Empire.* Philadelphia: The Jewish Publication Society of America, 1980.

Shapiro, Sidney, editor. *Jews in Old China.* New York: Hippocrene Books, 1984.

The illustrations in this book were done with graphite, colored pencil,

pastel, and watercolor on Arches watercolor paper.

The display type was set in Oxford.

The text type was set in Spectrum by Thompson Type, San Diego, California.

Color separations by United Graphic Pte. Ltd., Singapore

Printed and bound by Tien Wah Press, Singapore

This book was printed on totally chlorine-free Nymolla Matte Art paper.

Production supervision by Stanley Redfern and Ginger Boyer

Designed by Michael Farmer